CANTICLE OF THE CREATURES

*To our son Caoimhín, with love and thanks;
and to my companions in the Secular Franciscan Order
in Scotland, Wales and England*

St Francis'

Canticle of the Creatures

John Watts

with illustrations by
Caoimhín Watts

GRACEWING

First published in England in 2019

by

Gracewing

2 Southern Avenue

Leominster

Herefordshire HR6 0QF

United Kingdom

www.gracewing.co.uk

ISBN 978 085244 945 5

Typeset by Word and Page, Chester, UK

Front cover illustration by Caomhín Watts
Cover design by Bernardita Peña Hurtado

CONTENTS

PREFACE

My purpose in writing this short book has been two-fold: firstly, to provide a resource for Franciscans, in particular my companions in the Secular Franciscan Order, for possible use in formation and discussion; and secondly, to offer an introduction to Francis for others who may be interested in the saint. His *Canticle* is in fact an apt 'way in' to him, for as Chesterton pointed out nearly a century ago, it is 'a supremely characteristic work' and 'much of St Francis can be reconstructed from [it] alone.' [1]

In the vast literature on Francis and Franciscanism much has been written concerning his poem, and though most of it has been in Italian, French or German several valuable works have appeared in English. Of these the most important are by Murray Bodo, Eric Doyle, and Eloi Leclerc (in translation from the French). Each in its different way is highly thought-provoking, as well as deeply spiritual and Franciscan. Each takes its own approach to the *Canticle*, so that it largely complements the others and says much that is new and different. My own approach has been different again, so that those who have already read any or all of the above works should still find new ideas in this one.

Two other works should be mentioned here. On the specific issues of the *Canticle*'s place of composition and

[1]   G. K. Chesterton, *St Francis of Assisi* (London and Toronto, 1924), n.d., 103.

the precise meaning of one of its key words, an excellent summary has been provided by Raphael Brown. And on the particular theme of the Franciscan view of Creation, which inevitably touches on our subject, Sr Ilia Delio's book is to be highly recommended. (Publication details of all the above works may be found in the Suggestions for Further Reading on p. 71).

In seeking to grasp and express the meaning of the *Canticle* I have often turned to Scripture. The Old and New Testaments have been my main sources, indeed, and this is appropriate since these were always Francis' own main sources. As with every religious writer of his time Scripture informs all his writing; his works are dense with biblical allusions. His original Rule for the friars, for example, comprised little more than a series of excerpts from the Gospels.[2] And his *Canticle* is no exception. It contains no direct biblical quotations or references, certainly; rather, it is the free poetry of a man thoroughly versed in Scripture, which is his constant background companion.

The biblical passages quoted in the present work are based on the sixteenth- to seventeenth-century Douay-Rheims Bible, modernised, since this version is a direct English translation from the Latin Vulgate that Francis used. I have also sometimes quoted from the Vulgate itself, where this helped to draw out the meaning.

---

[2] This according to his near-contemporary and first biographer Thomas of Celano – 1 Celano, 32. The original Rule has not survived.

ACKNOWLEDGEMENTS

Among those who have helped in the making of this book I should particularly thank Attilio Galimberti OFS, Fr Edmund Highton OFM, Fr Robert Mann SCJ, Fraser Pearce, Silvana Puddinu, and especially Caoimhín Watts.

Canticle of the Creatures

1   Altissimu, omnipotente, bonsignore,
    tue sono le laude,
    la gloria elhonore
    et omne benedictione.

2   Ad te solo, Altissimo, se konfano
    et nullu homo enne dignu
    te mentovare.

3   Laudate sie, misignore, cum tucte le tue
        creature
    spetialmente messor lo frate sole,
    loquale iorno et allumini noi par loi.

4   Et ellu ebellu eradiante cum grande
        splendore:
    de te, Altissimo, porta significatione.

5   Laudato si, misignore, per sora luna ele
        stele:
    in celu lai formate clarite
    et pretiose et belle.

6   Laudato si, misignore, per frate vento,
    Et per aere et nubilo
    et sereno et omne tempo
    per loquale a te creature
    dai sustentamento.

1 Most high, all powerful, good Lord,
Yours are the praises,
the glory and the honour
and all blessing.

2 To You alone, Most High, do they belong,
and no man is worthy
to pronounce Your name.

3 Praised be You, my Lord, with all Your
creatures,
especially Sir Brother Sun,
who is day, and through him we are given
light.

4 And he is beautiful and radiant with great
splendour:
of You, Most High, he bears the likeness.

5 Praised be You, my Lord, through Sister
Moon and the stars:
in heaven they were formed, clear
and precious and fair.

6 Praised by You, my Lord, through Brother
Wind,
and through air both cloudy
and serene, and every weather,
by which all Your creatures
are given sustenance.

7 Laudato si, misignore, per sor aqua,
laqale e multo utile e humile
et pretiosa et casta.

8 Laudato si, misignore, per frate focu,
per loquale ennalumini la nocte:
edello ebello et iocundo
et robustoso et forte.

9 Laudato si, misignore, per sora nostra
matre terra,
laquale ne sustenta et governa,
et produce diversi fructi
con coloriti flori et herba.

10 Laudato si, misignore, per quelli ke
perdonano
per lo tuo amore
et sostengo infirmitate
et tribulatione.

11 Beati quelli kel sosterrano in pace,
ka da te, Altissimo,
sirano incoronati.

12 Laudato si, misignore, per sora nostra
morte corporale,
da laquale nullu homo
vivente poskappare.

7   Praised be You, my Lord, through Sister
        Water,
    who is very useful and humble
    and precious and chaste.

8   Praised be You, my Lord, through Brother
        Fire,
    by whom you light up the night:
    and he is beautiful and playful
    and robust and strong.

9   Praised be You, my Lord, through our
        Sister Mother Earth,
    who sustains and governs us,
    and who brings forth diverse fruit
    with coloured flowers and herbs.

10 Praised be You, my Lord, through those
        who pardon
    for Your love
    and bear infirmity
    and tribulation.

11 Blessed those who endure in peace,
    for by You, Most High,
    they shall be crowned.

12 Praised be You, my Lord, through our
        Sister
    bodily Death,
    from whom no man
    living can escape.

13 Gai acqueli ke morrano
ne le peccata mortali!

14 Beati quelli ke trovarane
le tue sanctissime voluntati,
ka la morte secunda
nol farra male.

15 Laudate et benedicite misignore,
et rengratiate et servaite li
cum grande humilitate.

13 Woe to those who die
    in mortal sin!

14 Blessed those whom death will find
    in Your most holy will,
    for the second death
    will not do them harm.

15 Praise and bless my Lord,
    and give him thanks, and serve Him
    with great humility.

Perhaps you have skipped over the Umbrian version, reader? If so, do go back and read it. There are several things in the *Canticle* that can only really be understood with their full meaning in the language in which they were composed. And in any case, enjoy the music of it!

❋ The Background ❋

THE *Canticle of the Creatures* is a praise poem, addressed – apart from the final verse – directly to God. It was composed towards the end of Francis' life, when he was almost blind and very ill (so it is thought) with tuberculosis. It was composed in three parts, at three different times, which, though they all concern praise, are distinct in subject, tone and style. The main body of it, comprising verses 1–9 and the final verse 15,[1] gives praise to God in His creation – it is this part that gives the whole its title. The second, verses 10–11, praise Him in those who give pardon and endure tribulation. The third, verses 12–14, praise Him in death.

Poems are often occasioned by particular events or experiences in the life of the poet, and it is thus with the *Canticle*. Verses 1–9 and 15 were composed in the early autumn of 1225 at St Clare's convent at San Damiano. Francis, now seriously ill, was resting in a hut of reeds built for him in the grounds by the sisters. Early sources state that he had a vision one night in which God spoke to him about his infirmity

---

[1]   Most English versions (including the most recent standard edition of Francis' works, R. J. Armstrong, J. A. W. Hellmann and W. J. Short (eds.), *Francis of Assisi: Early Documents*, New York 1999, vol. 1 pp. 113f) comprise fourteen verses. Fifteen are used here to correspond with the earliest version of the Umbrian original.

and tribulation and promised him a place in heaven.[2] In the morning the saint called his friars together and said to them, 'the Lord has deigned to promise me that I shall one day enter His Kingdom. So to show Him my gratitude I wished to compose this new song.'

He was prompted to write verses 10–11 after a quarrel had broken out between the bishop of Assisi and the Podesta of the town[3], probably in September 1225. He arranged for some of the brothers to sing the *Canticle* with the new verses added at the bishop's palace in the presence of the two men. So moved were they that they embraced and begged each other's forgiveness

Francis composed verses 12–14 on death in late September 1226, when it was known that his own death was near. Witnesses tell us that he called two of his closest companions, Brothers Angelo and Leo, to his sick bed and asked them to sing the *Canticle* to him. When they had reached the verses on pardon he stopped them and himself added the three new verses. They then sang the final verse together; it was the first time that the *Canticle* as we know it was sung in its entirety. On 3 October Francis died.

Thus the incidents that inspired the poem were specific and personal. They were directly personal in the case of the verses on enduring infirmity and tribulation, and those on death; while even those on pardon were indirectly so, in that the quarrel between Assisi's two most prominent men was hurting Francis' city.

---

[2] 2 Celano, 213 in M. H. Habig (ed.), *Omnibus of Sources*, Chicago 1983, 532f.

[3] Podesta – the chief Magistrate or civil Governor.

His 'take' on the Creatures (verses 3–9) was also unique and very much his own. The whole *Canticle*, in short, is deeply personal, so much so that I believe no one else could have composed it as it is.

Nevertheless, though the incidents that prompted it were particular and personal to him, that is not how he wrote it. On the contrary, its approach is general and universal. It is not about Francis considering God's creation and praising Him – nowhere is there any sign of the first person singular;[4] it is not Francis urging pardon to mend a particular quarrel in Assisi, not Francis who endures infirmity and tribulation and faces death: it is Everyman.

The *Canticle of the Creatures* is generally considered the earliest poem of standing to have been written in the Italian language. In nearly all anthologies of Italian literature, where works are presented in chronological order, it will be found on the first page.

Francis chose to use the vernacular for his poem, rather than Latin which would have been the more obvious choice. There was already a wealth of religious writing in that language, including many fine hymns in use in the Church, some composed as early as the fourth century. He had been raised on these Latin works and knew them well.

---

[4]   Compare in contrast the well loved hymn of praise (itself a kind of modern 'Canticle of the Creatures') 'O Lord my God, when I in awesome wonder/Consider all the works Thy hands have made....Then sings my soul, my Saviour God to Thee/How great Thou art....'

There was also a long tradition of secular verse in the language, dating back to the great poets of antiquity. But all such poetry was bound by and composed according to strict rules of Rhetoric, and in style is quite unlike the *Canticle*. It clearly had no influence upon Francis' composition. Indeed, it is unlikely that he was very familiar with Latin secular poetry, for he readily admitted to being *illiteratus*,[5] that is, one not versed in the classical authors.

It was a conscious decision on his part to compose his work in the vernacular, the *lingua volgare*, which in his day was only beginning to be thought of as a worthy medium for serious poetry. Elsewhere in Europe, in the Germanic speaking lands, there had long been a flourishing vernacular literature. Fine poetry had been composed in Anglo-Saxon, for instance, since about 700. But because they developed from Latin the Romance languages emerged later; and because of Latin's pre-eminence as the medium for poetry and prose, they were late in being accepted as fit for serious literature. Old French and Provençal were the first to be so.

In Umbria two distinct genres of vernacular poetry had become established shortly before Francis' birth. The first was the verse of the Troubadours, the minstrels who wandered across Western Europe composing and singing their love songs. The genre had originated in Provence, and Provençal was the normal language

---

[5] *Mirror of Perfection*, 64. The word does not carry our modern meaning 'illiterate'.

of composition.[6] We know that Francis understood Provençal, that in his youth he had admired the Troubadours' poetry, and that after he had founded his Order of friars he sent some of them out among the people to preach by singing, as 'jongleurs of God'.[7] And where the Troubadours composed poems in praise of their ladies, he was composing one in praise of his Lord. We might suppose, therefore, that their poetry could be his natural model. But again, this is not so. Though he is conventionally called 'God's Troubadour', the influence of the minstrels upon his *Canticle* was minimal. They may have played some small part in his choosing to compose in the vernacular, but they had no influence upon its actual composition. His theme has nothing in common with theirs. Nor does he owe anything to their style, which is typically sophisticated and mannered in its use of conceits and other literary devices, and at times even deliberately enigmatic. Usually it is rhymed. His poem on the contrary is simple, direct, quite close to the spoken language, and unrhymed.

If we are looking for models and sources of influence, we must look elsewhere. And our key is in the titles given to his poem in his day. He himself called

---

[6] By Francis' day some troubadour poetry was also beginning to be composed in several of the local dialects of Italy.

[7] *Legend of Perugia*, 43. One of his friars, Brother Pacifico, had been a noted Troubadour. As a religious Francis rejected the 'courtly love' that is the basis of the Troubadours' poetry, which (though addressed from afar to the idealised and unattainable lady) was extra-marital and often adulterous in aspiration. But he still admired their chivalric code of 'courtesy', a Christian code of behaviour that was far more wide-ranging than our modern word suggests.

it a 'canticle'; many of his near-contemporaries called it *Laudes Creaturarum*: both names are pointers to the sources that had the most important influence upon it.

We will take the latter name first. The *Laudes* (or *Laude* in Umbrian, as in modern Italian) were the second of the vernacular poetic genres that had become established in Umbria shortly before Francis' birth, and with which he was familiar. They were religious poems and, as their name tells us, usually composed in praise of God or the saints. Francis' *Canticle* was one of the early *Laude*. It was composed as such – as a praise poem, in which the word 'praise' in one form or another (*laude, laudato, laudate*) appears more than any other and is the key word, the *leitmotif*.

Francis' *Lauda* was to have an important place in the subsequent history of the genre. The renown of its author and the rapid spread of the religious Orders that he founded played a major part in ensuring the growth in popularity of *Laude* across Italy and elsewhere in Europe.[8]

Laude were composed to be sung. Their music was monophonic, and may well have been influenced by the songs of the Troubadours, for similarities have been noted between the two in regard to rhythm, melodic line and notation.

---

[8] Including England. Perhaps its greatest exponent was the poet Jacopone da Todi, himself a Franciscan. The *Laude* in turn led to the development of two other very different religious forms, the Medieval religious drama and (at a later date) the Oratorio.

We turn now to Francis' own title for his poem — 'Canticle'. The word was first used as a term to denote a song in the Comedies of the ancient Roman theatre. From the earliest days of Christianity the Church in the Latin West adopted it to mean a sacred song, of which numerous examples were found in Scripture. In the Old Testament the 'Canticle of Canticles' comprises a whole book in itself;[9] among other examples perhaps the best known are Moses' song of victory after leading the Jewish people through the Red Sea (Exod. 15: 1–19) and the song of the three young men in the furnace (Dan. 3: 52–90, of which more later). In the New Testament probably the most familiar canticle is Mary's song in the house of her cousin Elizabeth, known as the Magnificat (Luke 1: 46–55).

Francis knew his Bible, and it informed all his thinking. He gained his knowledge particularly through the Divine Office of the Church, which largely comprised psalms, canticles and other scriptural readings, as well as hymns, and which he as a religious recited daily.

We know that in the ancient Jewish tradition, canticles and psalms were set to music and 'sung' to the accompaniment of instruments such as the harp, timbrel, horn and cymbals.[10] It is thought that the music was not unlike Plainchant, and that in this form it was adopted by the early Christians.[11] From the out-

---

[9] Vulg. *Canticum Canticorum*. More familiar today as the 'Song of Songs'.

[10] Several of the Psalms make reference to such instruments.

[11] One early stringed instrument of the Christian era, the Psaltery, actually took its name from the fact that it was used to accompany recital of the psalter.

set canticles and psalms were chanted in the Church's liturgy, and only hymns sung. After the regularising of the Divine Office during the pontificate of Gregory the Great (590–604), this musical form came to be known as 'Gregorian Chant'.

Thus in their different ways both Canticles and *Laude* were composed to be set to music. For Francis to name his poem a 'Canticle', therefore, and for some contemporaries to give it the title *Laudes Creaturarum*, shows that they did not see it as a poem merely but as musical in some way. Early sources tell us that he or one of the brothers composed a tune for it, or perhaps adapted an existing one, and also that he wished it to be 'sung' by the brothers. As we saw, it was 'sung' on his death bed.

It is not known what music was adopted for it. Probably it was that of a *Lauda* rather than a Canticle, a song rather than a chant. It is quite possible to fit a melody to it, though because of the variation of the length of its verses this would require the repetition of some lines or phrases. On the other hand, it also fits neatly as it stands for recitation as Gregorian Chant (see Appendix 1).

Whatever precisely its music was, it was certainly composed to be 'sung' in some form. And it is still being sung to this day. In Franciscan parishes in Italy it is often sung as a hymn at Mass. Versions of it, more or less close to the original, have appeared as songs in several Italian Musicals,[12] while the film *Fratello Sole Sorella Luna*[13] includes a free adaptation of it, with different words but a similar theme. Over the years it has been set to music by numerous composers both classical and popular. Franz Liszt in the nineteenth century and William Walton in the twentieth are only two among a number of classical musicians who have composed for it. It has been adapted as a hymn in many languages, Draper's 'All Creatures of our Lord and King' being the version most familiar to English speakers. It has even inspired the folk singer Donovan to compose a song 'Brother Sun and Sister Moon' based very loosely upon it. All of these in their different ways attest not only to the poem's musical origins but to the fact that it is 'musical' in its very being – as was its author, of course, who (it is said) often danced upon the road and sang his way journeying through the Marches of Ancona.[14]

If, as seems most likely, the *Laude* gave Francis' poem its music, the Canticles and psalms of the Daily Office were the main sources for its theme. And among the different Hours that make up the Office it was Lauds that provided a special influence. This Office is recited at dawn, and though every Hour includes praise of God, Lauds (as its name suggests) is the praise Office

---

[12] The first of these was *Forza Venite Gente*, 1981, in which the *Canticle* (in modern Italian) forms the closing song.

[13] Directed by F. Zefferelli, 1972. The version in the film is '*Dolce sentire*'.

[14] *Three Companions*, IV, 33.

par excellence. Not surprising, therefore, that we should find in it the most important and direct sources for Francis' praise poem.

Traditionally the Office of Lauds comprised psalms, canticles and other prayers common throughout the year, as well as hymns etc. proper to the feasts and seasons of the liturgical calendar. Among the former, those that we need to look at are two of the *Laudate* psalms, nos. 148 and 149, particularly the first[15]; the Canticle of the Three Young Men in the Furnace (Dan. 3: 52–90), known as the Benedicite; and the Canticle of Zechariah at the naming of John the Baptist (Luke 1: 68ff), the Benedictus.

The first to mention is Psalm 149, whose influence was minor but, I believe, telling. We recall that on the morning after his vision Francis told the brothers that he wished to make a new song in praise of the Lord for His creatures.[16] The opening verse of Psalm 149 reads

Sing to the Lord a new Canticle.

It seems completely in character for the saint, and his literal approach to Scripture, that he would take the psalmist's imperative 'sing' literally as an injunction for himself to compose his own new canticle of praise.[17]

---

[15] Psalms 148–50 are known as the *Laudate* psalms. They are the last three psalms in the psalter, and all are included in the Office of Lauds.

[16] This version of his words is from *Mirror of Perfection* 100.

[17] He might have found a similar 'command' elsewhere in the Old Testament – eg., Psalm 95, Isaiah 42: 10, Judith 16: 2, etc.

By far the most important influences upon his poem, however, were the Benedicite and the Laudate Psalm 148. The similarity between these two sources and his work is so striking that it barely requires comment. I quote below only those verses that have a direct bearing on the *Canticle*.

Benedicite (Daniel 3: 52, 57, 62–78):

> Blessed are You Lord God of our fathers, worthy to be praised and glorified and exalted above all for ever....
>
> All you works of the Lord, bless the Lord: praise and exalt Him above all for ever....
>
> You sun and moon, bless the Lord: praise and exalt Him above all for ever.
>
> You stars of heaven, bless the Lord: praise and exalt Him above all for ever.
>
> Every shower and dew, bless the Lord: praise and exalt Him above all for ever.
>
> All you spirits of God, bless the Lord: praise and exalt Him above all for ever.
>
> You fire and heat, bless the Lord: praise and exalt Him above all for ever.
>
> You cold and heat, bless the Lord: praise and exalt Him above all for ever.
>
> You dews and frosts, bless the Lord: praise and exalt Him above all for ever.
>
> You frost and cold, bless the Lord: praise and exalt Him above all for ever.
>
> You ice and snow, bless the Lord: praise and exalt Him above all for ever.
>
> You nights and days, bless the Lord: praise and exalt Him above all for ever.

You light and darkness, bless the Lord: praise and
exalt Him above all for ever.
You lightnings and clouds, bless the Lord: praise and
exalt Him above all for ever.
Let the earth bless the Lord: let it praise and exalt
Him above all for ever.
You mountains and hills, bless the Lord: praise and
exalt Him above all for ever.
All that springs up in the earth, bless the Lord: praise
and exalt Him above all for ever.
You fountains, bless the Lord: praise and exalt Him
above all for ever.
You seas and rivers, bless the Lord: praise and exalt
Him above all for ever.

Laetare (Psalm 148: 1–3, 7–9):

Praise the Lord from the heavens: praise Him in the
high places.
Praise Him all His angels, praise Him all His hosts.
Praise Him sun and moon, praise Him all you stars
and light ...
Praise the Lord from the earth, you dragons and all
you deeps:
Fire and hail, snow, ice, stormy winds, which fulfil
His word:
Mountains and all hills, fruitful trees and all cedars.[18]

Finally from the Office of Lauds, we must point to two
verses from the Canticle of Zechariah (Luke 1: 68–79)
which have an important if indirect bearing on Francis'
poem: this will be discussed later in Appendix 2.

---

[18] The call to created things to praise the Creator may be found, expressed
briefly, elsewhere in the Psalms: Ps 102: 22 'Bless the Lord, all his works';
Ps 144: 10 'Let all your works praise You, O Lord'.

Elsewhere in the Church's liturgy, among the devo-
tions proper to particular feasts and seasons, we find
a hymn used in Advent, *Jubilemus omnes*, dating from
the twelfth century, that was also doubtless in Francis'
mind when he composed his *Canticle*.[19] Below is a
translation of its first eight verses:

Jubilemus Omnes (verses 1–8, of 12):

> Let us all sing together with joy to our God
> Who created all things;
> Through Whom the ages were founded:
> the heaven that shines with abundant light
> and the multitude of stars;
> The sun, fashion of the world,
> the moon, ornament of the night,
> and all bright things;
> The sea, the land, the heights, the plains,
> and the deep rivers;
> The wide expanses of the air, through which
>   birds speed,
> the winds and the rain.
> These things all together, God our Father,
> march to Your command alone,
> Now and for ever,
> through the ages, without end.
> Their praise is Your glory.

---

[19] The relevance of this hymn for the *Canticle* was first pointed out by
Raphael Brown (Appendix VIII in Englebert O., Chicago 1965, 441); Brown,
however, does not quote the words of the hymn. The present translation is
my own. The hymn was used on Thursday of the 3rd week of Advent.

If the similarities between the above sources and Francis' *Canticle* are clear, so also are the differences. Where the Benedicite and Psalm 148 address Creation his poem is addressed directly to God. Where they merely mention the created things, listing them like a litany, he pictures them and gives each a vivid description. The *Jubilemus* addresses the faithful, and from verse 6 God, and its descriptions of created things are brief and little more than labels. In Francis' hands they come to life, and take on their own life.

He calls them *creature*.[20] In his day the word could either mean 'creatures' in our sense of the word, or 'created things'. He was thus able to use it quite naturally for inanimate things, the sun, the moon, water, etc.[21] None of his 'creatures' is animate. And yet — unlike in his models – they *are* animate: alive, sentient, active. They are creatures in our sense of the word; in fact, they are more than creatures: they are *people*.

A further telling difference between the *Canticle* and its models lies in the way that the creatures praise God, and their relationship with Him. Here we need to look at Francis' use of two small and seemingly harmless prepositions. The first occurs in verse 3: 'Be praised, my Lord, with all Your creatures'. We could easily pass over this, but by the word 'with' (*cum*) Francis tell us that God is to be praised along with what He has created. Creation itself is praised, not of course as God's

[20] The Umbrian word has four syllables: cre-a-tur-e.

[21] Though most English versions of the poem translate 'tucte le tue creature' as 'all Your creatures', several including Habig (p. 130), prefer 'all that You have made.'

equal, but still with Him. In this one word Francis is giving a powerful affirmation of the material world, an affirmation the more striking when we remember that in his day and for many centuries before him, Christian contemplatives seeking spiritual perfection had often been led to reject and even despise the material world. He on the contrary was deeply aware that that world is the work of God, in Whose eyes every created thing is good.[22]

The second preposition, *per*, occurs throughout the *Canticle*, and its use has been the subject of much debate. In the Umbrian of the early thirteenth century it had at least three possible meanings – 'for', 'by' and 'through'. Which one is Francis using here? Is he praising God *for* the things He has created, for creating them and giving them to us? Or is he saying that God is praised *by* (or *through*) them, that they give Him praise by their existence, through being what they are and doing what they do? His models the Benedicite and Psalm 148 only carry the second meaning. Many modern scholars believe that Francis intended both.[23]

In all these ways, though his theme owes much to that of his antecedents, the *feel* of his poem is quite different. He does not follow his sources mechanically. Rather, he is apparently so familiar with them that he

[22] Cf. Gen. 1: 31.

[23] For a summary of the debate see R. Brown, Appendix VIII of O. Englebert 1965; also R. J. Armstrong, J. A. W. Hellmann and W. J. Short (eds.), 1999, 114 note a.

has thoroughly interiorised them and can use them in his own way.

There is evidence, also, that he had pondered his theme over a period of time before composing the *Canticle*. At some earlier time he had composed his own 'Praises', for recitation by the brothers before each Hour of the Daily Office.[24] They run to eleven verses, which include the following:

2   O Lord our God, You are worthy to receive praise, glory and honour and blessing.
Let us praise and glorify Him for ever ...

5   Bless the Lord, all you works of the Lord;
let us praise and glorify Him for ever ...

7   Let heaven and earth praise Him, Who is glorious;
let us praise and glorify Him for ever.

8   Every creature in heaven, on earth and under the earth,
and in the sea and those which are in it.
Let us praise and glorify Him for ever.

These verses sound like an early embryo of the *Canticle*, later to be developed and filled out.

---

24 Though undated they were certainly composed before the *Canticle*.

Nor was his use of the terms 'Brother' and 'Sister' new to his poem. He used them frequently in a similar way in life. He addressed 'Brother Fire' at the time when his eyes were to be cauterised, for example; and he famously referred to his own body as 'Brother Ass'.

In short, though his *Canticle* is assuredly a spontaneous creation, its original verses being composed swiftly in one dawn, the germ of it had perhaps been in his mind for some time.

We have given recognition to the sources that must have inspired Francis. But we must also recognise that he created something quite original. His is a unique work, a Canticle like no other. And this, after all, is what we would expect of the man. Among all his extraordinary spiritual gifts, one that should not be forgotten is his originality. He was one of the most original men known to history. He looked at everything, whether Scripture or the world around him, always with fresh eyes.

✳ The 'Creatures' Verses ✳

HAVING LOOKED AT THE CONTEXT and background of the *Canticle*, we will now consider it briefly verse by verse.

1   Most High, all powerful, good Lord,
    Yours are the praises,
    the glory and the honour
    and all blessing.

2   To You alone, Most High, do they belong,
    and no man is worthy
    to pronounce your name.

These two opening verses comprise a Doxology, an expression of praise for God. They create a solemn opening to the *Canticle*. Their tone is impressive even in translation, but may be appreciated best in the original, with its rhythms and sonorous vowel sounds.

Francis had begun his 'Praises to be Said at all the Hours' with a rather similar Doxology, also of two verses. Praise of God's glory was at the heart of his spiritual life, and is to be found at every turn in his writings.[1] This is, of course, exactly in line with the practice of the Church, throughout whose liturgy the praise of God recurs constantly. In the Divine

---

[1]   See among others his *Exposition on the Our Father*, *Exhortation to the Praise of God*, and *The Praises of God*.

Office, for instance, the Lesser Doxology – 'Glory to the Father, and to the Son, and to the Holy Spirit ' – concludes every psalm and canticle. And the Mass for Sundays and Solemnities always includes the Great Doxology – 'Glory to God in the Highest … We praise You, we bless You, we adore You, we glorify You, we give You thanks for Your great glory …' In these brief words, which Francis was brought up on, appear all the key elements of his *Canticle* – praise, blessing, and (in the final verse of his poem) thanks.

Scripture too afforded him numerous such formulae of praise. There are several in the Letters of the New Testament, for instance, where they often come at the beginning of the letter and serve as an introduction to it, setting the scene for its contents.[2] This is precisely how Francis uses his Doxology – it sets the theme for the whole poem.

Well known doxologies were to be found in both the Old and New Testaments – in the Old Testament, in 1 Chronicles 29: 10–11, for instance;[3] or in the New in Revelation 4: 11, where the words are quite close to his own – 'You are worthy, O Lord our God, to receive glory and honour and power, because you have created all things.' In both of these examples God is given glory as the Creator of the universe, just as He is in the *Canticle*.

---

[2] As in Ephesians, 2 Corinthians and 1 Peter. In Romans and Jude they come at the end, rounding off the writer's message.

[3] 'Yours, O Lord, is magnificence, and power and glory and victory,/ for all that is in heaven and on earth is Yours'.

In verse 2 a new theme is introduced: 'no man is worthy to pronounce Your name'. Here Francis expresses a concept that pre-dates Christianity. In fact, it is almost as old as the Jewish people, and from an early date was deeply embedded in their culture. The theme originated at Moses' meeting with God at Horeb (Exodus, 3). When asked to tell His name God had answered 'I am Who am ... tell the people that 'Who is' sent you.' By this enigma, hidden in the word 'Yahweh', the Jews were to understand that God's name is incommunicable, and in time the pronouncing of it was strictly forbidden, except only by the High Priest on one day of the year within the Temple sanctuary. The proscription was a powerful expression of the ineffability of God.

This is Francis' theme in verse 2: a great gulf lies between the God of holiness and man; He is ineffable, 'most High and all powerful'. As well as praise and blessing, therefore, it is right to have 'Fear of the Lord', to recognise that we are not worthy even to speak His name.[4]

Thus the Doxology of Verses 1–2 expresses God's greatness and our unworthiness. These are the verses of a man of deep love for God and profound humility and 'poverty of spirit'. And that is exactly what we would expect of the Poverello, who made this the watchword of his own life and asked the same of his brothers.

---

[4] He had made a similar statement in Chap. 23 of his Earlier Rule of 1221.

3   Be praised, my Lord, with all Your
      creatures.

Francis now turns to creation, for (as we have seen)
the phrase 'all Your creatures' carries the meaning 'all
that You have created'. As in the Benedicite and the
Doxologies that we cited above, the Saint is praising
God for 'all that is in heaven and earth'. And like the
Benedicite and Psalm 148 he begins in heaven (with the
sun, moon and stars) and then moves to earth (with
wind, water, etc.)

However, whereas the Benedicite names many
things on our planet, both inanimate and living,
Francis names only four – wind and air, water, fire,
earth – and these are all inanimate (and this despite
his own famed love for living creatures). Clearly the
four are intended to be representative of all. Modern
science has to date identified 118 chemical elements,
from which everything on earth is made. The science
of the thirteenth century recognised only four – air,
water, fire and earth. In this sense, therefore, Francis'
four 'creatures' do indeed represent all.

All the creatures, though inanimate, are either male
or female. This may seem worthy of remark to the
English reader, for whom inanimate things are neuter and referred to as 'it'. But in Francis' Umbrian, of
course, as in modern Italian, there is no neuter gender;
everything is either masculine or feminine. Thus *sole*
(sun), *vento* (wind) and *focu* (fire) are 'he', and *luna ele
stele* (moon and the stars), *aqua* (water), and *terra* (earth)
are 'she'.

This was automatic for Francis. But there is also something very apt and right about it. For when languages were still in embryo and slowly being formed, the choice of gender was not random – it was mainly based on how people saw the character of things. In an important sense, in their character and action, sun, wind and fire were felt to be masculine, and moon, stars, water and earth feminine. Perhaps all ancient peoples thought of the sun as male, the moon as female, and the earth as our mother. It accorded with something deep in human nature.

3   (Praised be You, my Lord, with all Your
        creatures,)
    especially Sir Brother Sun,
    who is day, and through him we are given
        light.

4   And he is beautiful and radiant with great
        splendour:
    of You, Most High, he bears the likeness.

OF ALL HIS 'creatures', God is praised 'especially' with the sun. It is given pride of place in Francis' *Canticle*. Indeed, his own title for the poem was the 'Canticle of Brother Sun'. His contemporaries found the name unsatisfactory, a misnomer since the work is about far more than the sun alone. As we saw (p. 14 above), some gave it an alternative name, *Laudes Creaturarum*, the 'Praises of the Creatures'. Others preferred the 'Canticle of the Creatures', and this last name, though it still does not convey the poem's entire subject, has since their time usually been the preferred title. But Francis' choice of name shows the pre-eminence that he wished to give the sun in his *Canticle*.

He accords it pride of place because it bears the divine likeness. Like the Creator it is 'beautiful and radiant with great splendour'; and we might add, it is powerful, life-giving and life-sustaining, and 'everlasting'. In all these ways it appears to resemble God. But Francis is saying more than this. Though verse 4b is normally translated 'of You, Most High, he bears the likeness' (and this is perhaps the best single word we have in English), the poet's word *significatione* really means something like 'sign' as well as 'likeness'. Verse 4b is telling us that the sun is a metaphor for God. (The reader will find further discussion of the point in Appendix 2).

Francis speaks of the Sun with reverence, using the title *messor*. This word also is not readily translated in English. Some render it as 'my Lord', others as 'Sir', but neither is exactly right. In Medieval Italy *messor* (whose literal meaning is 'reaper') was reserved as a title for nobles of high lineage, so that from this point of view 'my Lord' is a fair approximation. But in the *Canticle* Francis already has the title 'My Lord' (*misignore*), which he reserves for God alone. For this reason 'Sir' would be a better translation, though its weakness is that it does not convey a high enough level of lineage and reverence.

In fact, the poet's full title for the Sun is *messor lo frate*, 'Sir brother'. It is a deliberately unlikely pairing of words, making the Sun at once his superior and his equal, distant yet close.

5   Praised be You, my Lord, through Sister
      Moon and the stars:
    in heaven they were formed, clear
    and precious and fair.

THE COSMOLOGISTS of Francis' day located all the heavenly bodies in eight concentric spheres circling the earth. The moon was in the first (that is, the lowest) sphere, the stars in the eighth and highest. Above them was a ninth sphere, which imparted motion to the rest. And above and beyond it lay the Empyrean, which did not move; it was heaven, the abode of God.

It was here, in heaven, Francis tell us, that the moon and stars were formed by God. Perhaps he pictured Him creating the stars as the psalmist imagined it, 'by the breath of His mouth',[5] and blowing them out across the sky.

He formed them 'clear and precious and fair'. The first descriptive adjective, *clarite*, linguists believe was actually coined by Francis himself. If so, surely he was trying to convey by it that peculiar, wonderful clearness that the moon and stars have on a frosty, cloudless night. The second adjective, *pretiose*, has the meaning 'of great price'. For Francis the Moon is like a 'pearl of great price', and the stars are like costly diamonds. But the word carries something of a personal and intimate meaning also – the Moon and stars are precious to Francis, just as something or someone loved is precious.

The three adjectives express Francis' sense of wonder as he pictures the Moon and Stars. But it is not the wonder of awe at their immensity and our seeming insignificance. Rather, it is the wonder of delight,

---

[5] Psalm 32: 6.

like that of a child who gazes into the night sky and is struck not by their vastness but their beauty. The saint is not concerned with their cosmic otherness. They are not remote; they are intimate, close; they are his sisters.

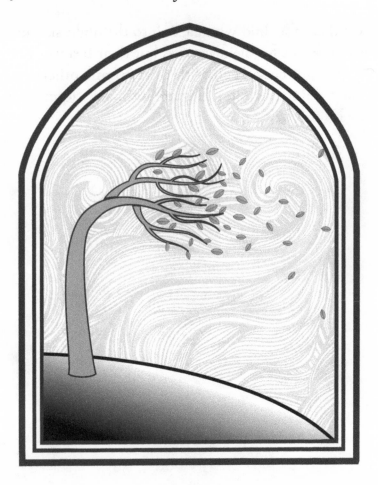

6   Praised be You, my Lord, through Brother
       Wind,
     and through air both cloudy
     and serene, and every weather,
     by which all Your creatures
     are given sustenance.

Francis gives us no description of the Wind, perhaps because it cannot be seen. He does not describe it, but instead tells us of its effects, what it does along with the air in its varied moods and every kind of weather. Where the Benedicite lists most of the weathers that one could think of, the *Canticle* offers no such exhaustive litany but covers them by the phrase *omne tempo*. All the vagaries of the weather, the pleasant and the unpleasant, are necessary to sustain God's creatures on the planet: cold and frost to break the earth, cloud and rain to water it, serene calm and warmth to make its seeds grow, flower and fruit.

7   Praised be You, my Lord, through Sister
      Water,
who is very useful and humble
and precious and chaste.

For WATER the poet again gives us descriptive adjectives. Firstly, it is 'useful'. With it we can be washed clean, or given life whether by drinking or by its watering the soil. The next three adjectives – 'humble, precious and chaste' – go together to describe Water's 'character'. Each is an unexpected choice, and for that reason telling and memorable. Water is 'humble', always taking the lowest way, running almost unseen as a little stream, and quietly getting on with its tasks. It is 'precious': here Francis perhaps partly means 'vital', as water is precious in a drought; but equally importantly he is conveying the sense of 'loved by us' for its own sake, rather as he has already used the word for the Moon and Stars: it has an intimate meaning. Lastly, Water is 'chaste'. Clean water is pure, and the poet might have used that word. But 'chaste' is far more striking and powerful. Whereas 'pure' can be used for inanimate or even abstract things, 'chaste' applies only to people. It is a solely human quality, and carries a moral intention. It is a far stronger, more 'active' word than 'pure'.

The adjectives are unexpected; yet they are exactly right. We can precisely picture Sister Water as a young woman. And the attributes that the poet ascribes to her – useful, humble, precious, chaste – are very Franciscan qualities.

8   Praised be You, my Lord, through Brother
     Fire,
   by whom You light up the night:
   and he is beautiful and playful
   and robust and strong.

IF WATER is a chaste young woman, Fire is a virile young man in the prime of life. He is handsome (the word *bello* is used for male as readily as *bella* for female) and with all his faculties. Francis' earliest biographer tells us that the saint had a special love for fire and said that it 'surpassed all other things in beauty'.[6] And another who knew him claimed that he disliked extinguishing even a flame or a candle, 'so moved was he with pity and love' towards them.[7]

Brother Fire is at the height of his physical strength (*robustoso*). But he is also playful (*iocundo*), with a glint of fun and maybe mischief in his eye. There is something of the lad about him, something of the Italian too, and we can imagine that as Francis pictured him he was partly thinking back to his own youth.

---

6   2 Celano, 166.

7   Writings of Leo, Ruffino and Angelo, 175.

9   Praised be You, my Lord, through our
      Sister Mother Earth,
who sustains and governs us,
and who brings forth diverse fruit
with coloured flowers and herbs.

IN THE DESCRIPTION OF THE SUN we remarked on Francis' striking use of two almost contradictory words 'Sir' and 'Brother' together. Here in writing of Earth as 'our Sister Mother' he uses a full-blown oxymoron! She is our sister, as all the creatures are our sister or brother. And she is our mother, in that she 'sustains and governs us'. Here again, Francis surprises with his choice of words. 'Sustains' we expect. But she also governs. She sets the rules, guides us, controls and limits what we can do. Perhaps the recognition that humanity is governed by earth, rather than earth being ruled by humanity, came more readily to a man of the thirteenth century than it does to us in the twenty-first. It certainly shows Francis' humility regarding our place in the world. In any case, we can be sure that his Earth is a kindly mother, governing us for our own good and wellbeing.

In the last two lines of this verse, 'who brings forth diverse fruit/ with coloured flowers and herbs', the reader may perhaps hear an echo of Genesis 1:11, where God commands the Earth to 'bring forth the green herb, and such as may seed, and trees yielding fruit each after its kind'. Is there not in Francis' description a hint of the Garden of Paradise?

❋ The Mystic ❋

INDEED, we may put a further question: is there not something ideal and innocent of harm in *all* his descriptions of the creatures? Never does he allude to the destructive possibilities of wind, water, fire and earth. He is aware of them, of course. But he only thanks God for their blessings.

A key passage from the work of the saint's biographer Thomas of Celano throws light on this question. The author, who clearly has the *Canticle* in mind, tells us that

> when [Francis] found an abundance of flowers, he preached to them and invited them to praise the Lord as though they were endowed with reason. In the same way he exhorted with the sincerest purity cornfields and vineyards, stones and forests and all the beautiful things of the fields, fountains of water and the green things of the gardens, earth and fire, air and wind, to love God and serve Him willingly. Finally, he called all creatures Brother, and in a most extraordinary manner, a manner never experienced by others, he discerned the hidden things of nature with his sensitive heart, as one who had already escaped into the freedom of the glory of the sons of God.[1]

---

[1]   1 Celano, 81.

In the last sentence of this passage Thomas makes a remarkable claim. He consciously echoes St Paul's words concerning the end of time, when 'the creation itself will be delivered from the servitude of corruption, into the freedom of the glory of the children of God' (Rom. 8: 21). Where now we see only darkly, Paul adds, then we shall see reality 'face to face'. Thus Thomas is here claiming that Francis, in a unique way not granted to others, was able to see into the hidden things of nature and discern the reality that we may all hope to see at the end of time. And, as his biographer realised, it was because he saw creation thus that 'he called all creatures Brother' (we should say, Brother and Sister).

Brother and Sister: two of the key words of the *Canticle*, and certainly the two most remembered. As poetry often does, they prompt us to see things in a new way. They encapsulate how Francis saw creation. He might have spoken of 'Sir Sun' or 'Miss Moon', but in calling them Brother and Sister he makes them part of a family, along with every other created thing including ourselves.

A family is a close group. Its members are precious to one-another, and dependent upon one-another. Each member shares the others' good and ill fortune, joys and sorrows. When one is hurt, all are hurt. All have equal dignity. A family is held together by love.

Thus Francis is saying that all created things are precious and beautiful; all are our fellows, all interdependent. Humankind is not superior. Creation is *one*, held together by God's love.

The Italian poet Dante, writing less than a century after Francis and himself a Third Order Franciscan, has a beautiful image for this concept. In the final canto of his *Paradiso* he recalls how he had ascended to the highest heaven and gazed into the eternal light of God. There he saw 'how it contains within its depths/ all things bound in a single book by love/ of which creation is the scattered leaves'.[2]

St Bonaventure in his authorised biography of Francis offers a series of images equally striking: Francis, he writes, saw God in the works of His creation, in 'the footprints [He] impressed on things'. He continues:

> In every created thing he tasted the Goodness which is the source of all, as in so many rivulets. He perceived a divine harmony in the chords of power and activity given them by God, and like the prophet David he exhorted them all to praise God.[3]

Francis, that is, grasped the oneness of creation, its single harmonious music, and in his *Canticle* exhorted us to praise God as David had in the psalms.

Such images – the single book of creation; the footprints of God; creation as countless streamlets from a single wellspring; the divine melodic harmony of all things – attempt to express Francis' profoundly mystical vision of creation. In his *Canticle*, with the

2 Dante, *Paradiso*, 33, 85–7.
3 Bonaventure, *Major Life*, IX, 1.

economy of true poetry, this vision is captured in two words, 'Brother' and 'Sister'.

His view of creation long pre-dated the discovery of evolution, of course. He did not think in terms of an evolving planet, or an evolving universe, as we do. He took it as a given that all 'creatures', both animate and inanimate, had been created once for all at the beginning of time; in this sense they were static. And this, along with his Christian faith, in turn determined his sense of history, whose dynamic was quite different from that which prevails today. In the Christendom of his day there was little concept of the world moving continuously forward according to the laws of biology and the other sciences. Its history was conceived as following a path guided by Providence, one that began with Creation and continued with the Fall, followed by the pagan era (including God's intervention through the Chosen People); the life, death and resurrection of Christ (which was seen as the hinge of world history); thence the Christian era; the Second Coming, the Last Judgment and the end of time.[4]

Though the science of Francis' day may have been primitive by our standards – pre-evolutionary, and recognising only four elements, for example – his own intuition of Brotherhood and Sisterhood was strikingly modern. He grasped what our scientists are only

---

[4]   Today's Christians, of course, still hold this providential view of history, but the time scale is now quite different, with a different dynamic, and immensely longer.

now discovering – the interdependence of all things. And he grasped it half a millennium before the birth of modern science.

❋ The Later Verses ❋

10 Praised be You, my Lord, through those
    who pardon
    for Your love
    and bear infirmity
    and tribulation.

11 Blessed those who endure in peace,
    for by You, Most High,
    they shall be crowned.

As WE NOTED, these two verses, along with verses 12–14, were later additions to the original *Canticle*; and they have the feel of additions. Verse 10 opens just like those that come before it, certainly – 'Praised be You, my Lord'. But now the whole tenor changes entirely. Those through whom God is to be praised are in no way like the 'creatures' who precede them: now it is those who give pardon or bear infirmity and tribulation. For the first time the *Canticle's* subject is humankind; for the first time pain and suffering, sadness and harm enter the poem. The style and thrust are also quite new: the verses are giving a message.

The subject of the message is two-fold – giving pardon, and bearing infirmity and tribulation. At first sight it seems a strange combination. But both these things involve 'enduring in peace'; both dispel bitterness. As we know, both were topical for Francis at the time – the first occasioned by the quarrel between the bishop and the Podesta of Assisi, the second by his dream of God's promise of salvation to him in his 'infirmity and tribulation'. His putting this same phrase from his dream into the *Canticle*, and the assurance in verse 11 that those who endure in peace 'shall be crowned' (that is, shall attain salvation) are no coincidence.

The wording of this verse, 'blessed are those who.... for they shall be crowned', inevitably recalls the 'Blessed are those who ... for they shall ...' in Christ's Sermon on the Mount (Matt. 5: 1–12 and Luke 6: 20–3). More-over, the pardon, the bearing of tribulation and the enduring in peace of the *Canticle* are not unlike the 'blessed are the merciful ... those who mourn now ... and the peace makers' of the Beatitudes. It has often been remarked that the Sermon on the Mount turns the values commonly praised by society on their head, extolling a way of life often scorned by the world. Francis does the same in these verses, as indeed he did in his whole life. One modern commentator has well called the saint's spirituality 'the upside-down world of the Beatitudes'.[1]

Christ taught His disciples how to pray, and so left to us the perfect prayer, the 'Our Father'. In it He laid only one obligation upon us, to 'forgive those who trespass against us'. If this is the one obligation He wished to place upon us, in the one prayer He chose to leave us, it must be at the very heart of His message.

---

[1] H. Julian, *Living the Gospel – the Spirituality of St Francis and St Clare*, Oxford 2001, 78.

Pardoning others is the essence of Christian living. And in these verses Francis has homed in on it.

'Praised be You, my Lord,' he writes, through those who pardon 'for Your love' (*per lo tuo amore*). Here again we encounter the preposition *per*; and again it appears to carry more than one meaning. Francis seems to be saying, on the one hand, 'those who pardon *for* Your love', that is, 'for love of You'; and on the other, 'those who pardon *through* Your love', that is, it is only through God's love that we are able to pardon.

12   Praised be You, my Lord, through our
     Sister
   bodily Death,
   from whom no man
   living can escape.

13   Woe to those who die
   in mortal sin!

14   Blessed those whom death will find
   in Your most holy will,
   for the second death
   will not do them harm.

The only description that Francis gives Death is implicit in the title 'Sister'. To the reader the juxtaposing of the words 'Death', 'Sister' and 'praise' is jarring, shocking even. They express a sharp contradiction, intentionally so of course: it is part of the 'contradiction' of Christianity. The last thing we would naturally say about

Death is that it gives praise to God. To do so would demand of us the greatest faith and trust in Providence. Francis had such faith and trust; and his calling Death 'Sister' suggests that he saw it as a gentle thing. We are reminded of the words of his first biographer, who wrote that the saint 'accepted death singing'.[2]

At this point the *Canticle* moves to a theme that is akin to a homily – no living man can escape Death.... woe to those who die in mortal sin....blessed those whom Death will find in God's will. Preaching had always been a large part of Francis' life as a friar. Here it is as if, knowing that he himself was soon to die, he wished to give his fellow men and women one last message of repentance.

He tells us that those who die in God's holy will shall not be harmed by 'the second death'. This rather strange term comes from the Book of Revelation, where it refers to the eternal punishment that will be meted out at the Last Judgment at the end of time to those in mortal sin (Rev., espec. 20: 14–15 and 21: 8). Francis' image of bodily Death is entirely orthodox and in line with his Church's teaching: it is terrible to those in grave sin, but (despite the human sadness of it) a blessed thing to those in God's grace.

We have noted that verses 10–14 were additions, and that they have that feel. They do not sit at one with the rest of the *Canticle*. Yet they add much to it. They give it new dimensions and new horizons. With them

---

[2] 2 Celano, 214.

included, the *Canticle* now embraces not only all created things, but man and his destiny on earth and
beyond. They complete the picture. Francis' poem
now spans creation, life, death, and eternity.

15 Praise and bless my Lord,
    and give Him thanks, and serve Him
    with great humility.

The *Canticle* began with a Doxology; it ends with an
Exhortation. Together the two form a 'frame' for the
poem. In this final verse it is no longer God who is
addressed, but ourselves. The theme is still praise and
blessing, but now in the imperative mood: *Laudate
et benedicite*. The Umbrian words echo to the letter
the Latin Laudate and Benedicite of Lauds which so
influenced Francis' composition.

To praise and blessing the saint now adds three more
themes – thanks, service and humility. First, thanks. It
is remarkable that in all his sickness and pain he seems
to have been aware only of his blessings. Some of us
may have been fortunate enough to meet someone
like that in life – the victim of an accident, crippling
disease or disability, perhaps – who thinks only of
his/her blessings. Such people are an inspiration; we
never forget them and we are the better for having
known them.

'Thanks' seems to have been one of the driving
forces of the *Canticle*. Francis told his brothers that
he had composed it 'because people are not grateful

for God's creatures'.[3] *He* was grateful; he thanked God. And in its final verse he bids us do the same.

Service was at the heart of his life, and of the lives of his brothers whom he urged to be 'the servants of all',[4] in imitation of Christ who came not to be served but to serve.[5] And although here in the *Canticle* he speaks only of serving God, surely he intends the words 'serve Him' to also imply serving God in serving our neighbour.

Francis asks us to serve Him 'with great humility'. Elsewhere he tells us that humility is the 'sister' of poverty, that the two are inseparable.[6] Interior poverty, 'poverty of spirit', is but an aspect of our humility before God. And few have ever served Him with greater humility than the Poverello.

Praise and blessing, gratitude, and service in humility – this final verse offers as good a summary as one could find of the Franciscan ideal. It tells us in a single sentence the essence of what Francis lived for. And it perfectly rounds off his *Canticle*.

---

3   This in the account in *Mirror of Perfection*, 100.
4   Letter to the Faithful, 2nd version, 47.
5   Mark 10: 45.
6   Salutation of the Virtues, 2.

❊ The Poem ❊

FRANCIS TOLD HIS BROTHERS that he wished to make a new song. He succeeded. Nothing quite like it had ever been composed before. It is new for us, also: like all true poetry it lets us see the world in a way that we had not previously seen it. He also explained to the brothers what had prompted him to compose his song. He did so, he told them, for 'God's glory, for our consolation, and for the edification of our neighbours'.[1]

God's glory came foremost. As to the 'consolation' of himself and the brothers, the choice of word is unusual but perhaps he simply meant the spiritual consolation gained by praising God. The third motive, to edify others, that is, to strengthen or build them spiritually, was in line with much Medieval religious poetry. We should not forget this element of edification in the *Canticle*. Verses 10–14 sound not unlike a sermon, the Creatures give us the example of virtue, and the poem as a whole seeks to give us spiritual sustenance.

There is little attempt at style in it; it is not literary. Its words and patterns are not far from those of speech. It is simple and spontaneous, and nowhere obscure. Indeed, how could it be otherwise? Here as in all his writings Francis wrote as he lived. In the best sense, his poem has something of the 'poverty' of the man.

---

[1] *Mirror of Perfection*, 100.

At the same time, it is written with assurance. He is so inspired by his theme that it carries its own eloquence.

For all its spontaneity, there are in it a few small signs of poetic crafting. It has often been pointed out, for instance, that the Creatures – Sun, Moon and stars, Wind, Water, Fire and Earth – are not arranged randomly, but symmetrically following a sequence alternating between male and female. Again, though the poem does not employ rhyme it makes use of assonance (in which the main vowel, and often other vowels of a word, rather than the entire word, rhymes with another close by).[2] Italian (in its various dialects) was especially well fitted for the use of this poetic device, because of the prominence of vowels in the language, and especially its use of vowel endings to indicate gender and number. The *Canticle* makes much use of assonance, both within-line (*utile et humile*), and especially end-of-line (*vento ... tempo ... sustentamento*; *aqua ... casta*; *mortali ... voluntati ... male*, etc.) The final verse includes the couple *rengratiate ... humilitate*, which is virtually a full rhyme and aptly emphasises the rounding off of the poem. The frequency of this device exceeds what would naturally occur in speech. Nonetheless, its use is such that the poem's 'feel' remains more that of spontaneity than art.

The *Canticle* is suffused with joy and hope. One modern biographer has described it as 'the most opti-

---

[2]　The poetry of several of the Romance languages of the day made use of assonance, notably Old French and Provençal, both of which were familiar to Francis.

mistic song ever to spring from a human heart'.[3] This is not optimism in the loose, general sense in which the word is often used today, though; rather, it is the particular optimism of Christian hope. The poem is the work of a man of hope, a man at peace with God and with himself. It has the mark of one who has travelled far spiritually. It has serenity. Another modern writer has drawn a similar conclusion, I think, when he claims that Francis could only have written the *Canticle* at the end of his life, since 'it is a poem that crystalizes a lifetime of reconciliation and integration'.[4]

Yet for all this, it still has the wonder of youth. This was something that Francis never lost. We noted the childlike wonder in his description of the Moon and stars (pp. 36–7 above). We might now add that something of this quality runs through the whole poem (apart from the later additions). And again, this is in character. From the early biographies it is clear that there remained much of the child in Francis – in his wonder at the world around him, his literal approach to things, his freshness of vision, his innocence and simplicity.

There is a passage in the Book of Wisdom (13: 2–5) which is most apt in regard to this quality of the *Canticle*:

> the fire, or the wind, or the swift air, or the circle of
> the stars, or the great water, or the sun and moon
> ... if [men] were *delighted* with their great beauty

[3]   O. Englebert, 1967 ed., 319.

[4]   M. Bodo, 8.

> … let them know how much the Lord of them is
> more beautiful than they … or if they felt *wonder* at
> their power and effects, let them understand by them
> that He who made them is mightier than they. For
> by the greatness of the beauty, and of the creature,
> the Creator of them may be seen. *(present author's
> emphases)*

Francis sees his Creatures with delight and wonder; and at the same time, with reverence.

The final quality of the poem to which I draw attention is the light that is within it (again, apart from verses 10–14 whose tone is more sombre). Francis was hardly able to see or bear the light when he composed it, yet he put so much light into it. The verses seem transparent, lapidary, gem-like. They have the bright luminosity of enamel work, or of a Medieval illuminated Book of Hours. The whole *Canticle* is like Sister Moon and the stars – 'clear and precious and fair'; and like Sister Water it is limpid and flows joyously.

Appendix 1

The *Canticle of the Creatures* and Gregorian Chant

The psalms and canticles of Scripture normally comprise verses of two lines, or sometimes of three. In the latter case, the extra line, known as a 'Flex', does not come after the other two but precedes them. When written down the flex is marked by the sign †, while a ★ between the two lines of the couplet indicates that when recited there should be a brief pause between them. Here as an example is the first verse of Psalm 99:[5]

> Sing joyfully to God all the earth, †
> Serve the Lord with gladness; ★
> Come before Him with great joy.

When sung in plain (Gregorian) chant, the first line of the pair has a rising cadence, thus:

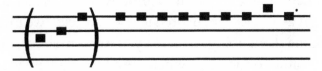

The second has a falling cadence:

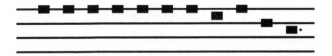

63

The Flex, if there is one, is a sharply falling line:

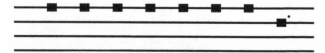

Since scansion of the lines is by stresses rather than syllables, the form allows for some variation in line length.

Gregorian Chant was devised for the Latin of the Western Church, and is most perfectly suited to that language, but it is adaptable to many forms of speech. The thirteenth century Umbrian of Francis' *Canticle*, being close to Latin, fits it particularly well. Moreover, the poem's themes fit neatly into verses of two or three lines (or combinations thereof). Thus for example Brother Sun has two verses, one of three lines and the other of two; the Moon and Stars have a single three line verse; Sister Bodily Death has three verses, etc.

When Gregorian Chant is used for the Divine Office by a monastic community, the two halves of the choir chant the verses alternately.[6] In a similar way, when shortly before his death Francis asked Brothers Angelo and Leo to sing his poem to him, (whether in fact they sang it as a *Lauda* or chanted it as a Canticle), we might imagine them doing so verse by verse turn-about, until they came to the place where he added his new verses on Sister Bodily Death, whereafter the three of them sang the final verse together.

For the reader's interest, the *Canticle* is set out below in Plain Chant notation. (Whereas the version used on pp. 2, 4, 6 of the present book, based on the earliest extant

---

[6] Occasionally the two halves chant groups of several verses alternately.

manuscript, has the poem divided into fifteen verses, the version used below[7] makes a different division, into thirteen verses. It also differs slightly from the other in line length, as well as in spelling, which was not standardised at this date. In fact, though, both versions fit the notation of Gregorian Chant equally well).

IL CANTICO DEL SOLE

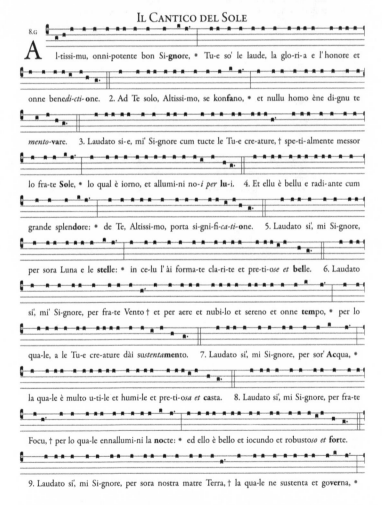

Al-tissi-mu, onni-potente bon Si-**gnore**, * Tu-e so' le laude, la glo-ri-a e l'honore et

onne ben*edi-cti-*one. 2. Ad Te solo, Altissi-mo, se konfano, * et nullu homo ène di-gnu te

*mento-*varce. 3. Laudato si-e, mi' Si-gnore cum tucte le Tu-e cre-ature, † spe-ti-almente messor

lo fra-te **Sole**, * lo qual è iorno, et allumi-ni no-*i per* lu-i. 4. Et ellu è bellu e radi-ante cum

grande splendore: * de Te, Altissi-mo, porta si-gni-fi-*ca-ti-*one. 5. Laudato si', mi Si-gnore,

per sora Luna e le **stelle**: * in ce-lu l'ài forma-te cla-ri-te et pre-ti-*ose et* **belle**. 6. Laudato

si', mi' Si-gnore, per fra-te Vento † et per aere et nubi-lo et sereno et onne **tempo**, * per lo

qua-le, a le Tu-e cre-ature dài su*stenta*mento. 7. Laudato si', mi Si-gnore, per sor' **Acqua**, *

la qua-le è multo u-ti-le et humi-le et pre-ti-o*sa et* **casta**. 8. Laudato si', mi Si-gnore, per fra-te

Focu, † per lo qua-le ennallumi-ni la **nocte**: * ed ello è bello et iocundo et robusto*so et* **forte**.

9. Laudato si', mi Si-gnore, per sora nostra matre Terra, † la qua-le ne sustenta et governa, *

[7] Kindly produced for the author on computer programme by Mr Fraser Pearce.

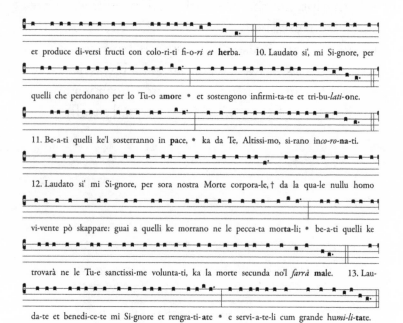

et produce di-versi fructi con colo-ri-ti fi-o-*ri et* **her**ba.   10. Laudato si', mi Si-gnore, per

quelli che perdonano per lo Tu-o **amore** • et sostengono infirmi-ta-te et tri-bu-*lati*-one.

11. Be-a-ti quelli ke'l sosterranno in **pace**, • ka da Te, Altissi-mo, si-rano in*co-ro-***na**-ti.

12. Laudato si' mi Si-gnore, per sora nostra Morte corpora-le,† da la qua-le nullu homo

vi-vente pò skappare: guai a quelli ke morrano ne le pecca-ta morta-li; • be-a-ti quelli ke

trovarà ne le Tu-e sanctissi-me volunta-ti, ka la morte secunda no'l *farrà* **male**.   13. Lau-

da-te et benedi-ce-te mi Si-gnore et rengra-ti-ate • e servi-a-te-li cum grande hu*mi-li-***ta**te.

OF YOU, MOST HIGH, HE BEARS THE LIKENESS

On p. 33 we mentioned some of the more obvious ways in which the sun bears a likeness to God, for which reason it has been likened to the divine in many religions, and even itself worshipped as a divinity. In the religion of the ancient Jewish people it very rarely appeared as a metaphor for Yahweh, perhaps in part in order to distance their religion from those of the Gentiles, including their captors in Egypt and Babylon, among whom sun worship was practised. The one striking use of the sun as metaphor for God in the Old Testament appears in Malachy, 4: 2, where the people are told 'to you who fear My name the Sun of Justice shall rise'.

In the New Testament the sun is made a metaphor for God by Zechariah at the time of the naming of his son John the Baptist, recounted by the evangelist Luke. In his canticle, known as the Benedictus and recited daily in the Office of Lauds, Zechariah speaks of God's forgiveness in these terms – 'through the bowels of the mercy of our God, in which the Rising Sun has visited us from on high' (Luke 1: 78).[8] Since Zechariah was speaking of his son John preparing the

[8] The Vulgate word 'Oriens' may be translated either as Rising Sun or Dawn; either translation involves the metaphor of the sun as God.

way for the Messiah, the first Christians easily took his image of the Sun to apply specifically to Christ. They remembered also that at the Transfiguration His face had 'shone like the sun' (Matt. 17: 2).[9] In particular, they associated the Rising Sun with Christ's rising from the dead, which had been witnessed by the women at dawn (Matt. 28: 1; Luke 24: 1).[10] Thus the Dawn/*Oriens* became a symbol of the Resurrection and man's salvation. Furthermore, it was from the East that Christ would come again. It became the practice for many early Christians to pray facing the dawn, to bury their dead likewise, and to erect crosses and build their churches facing east (*ad orientem*).

The Church Fathers dovetailed these concepts with the image of the Sun of Justice from Malachy, applying the latter explicitly to Christ the Rising Sun. The combined metaphor found its way into the liturgy of the Church, occurring in a number of hymns such as, for instance, the *Iam Christe Sol Justitiae* from the Office of Lauds.[11]

Closely related to the metaphor of God as the Sun is the image of God as Light. The Old Testament provides many examples of that image, of God as Light

[9] The accounts of the Transfiguration in Mark and Luke do not use this simile.

[10] Mark 16: 2 has 'very early in the morning'; John, 20: 1 has 'when it was still dark'.

[11] The opening lines read 'Now Christ, O Sun of Justice/ Let Dawn bless our darkened spirits'. This hymn may date from the time of St Ambrose (fourth century).

and the giver of light.[12] We find it more than once in the Psalms, for instance, and several times in Isaiah.

In the New Testament a crucial text for our purposes is again the Canticle of Zechariah, which brings the two images Sun and Light together. Zechariah's words that we quoted above – 'through the bowels of the mercy of our God, in which the Rising Sun has visited us from on high' – continue 'to enlighten those who sit in darkness and in the shadow of death'. Here Zechariah is consciously echoing a verse from Isaiah (9: 2): 'The people who walked in darkness have seen a great light; to those who dwelt in the shadow of death, light is arisen'. Isaiah's words were part of a passage prophesying the birth of a Messiah, and by echoing them Zechariah is making the same prophecy. Both men conceive of the Light rising as in the Dawn. And both are speaking of the Messiah bringing light to dispel spiritual as well as physical darkness.

The first Christians took from these texts the metaphor of Christ as Light enlightening a world darkened by sin. After all, had He not called Himself 'the light of the world' and promised that anyone following Him would no longer walk in darkness but would have the light of life (John 8: 12)? The image was given an important place in the liturgy of the Church. Most notably, the faithful heard it at Mass in the Creed where Christ is 'God from God, Light from Light'. They found it too in the Divine Office, in a number

---

[12] Light was in fact God's first creation – Gen., 1: 3.

of hymns addressed to the Son in the dawn Office of Lauds, hymns such as *Splendor Paternae Gloriae*:

> Splendour of the Father's glory,
> bringing light from light,
> Light of Light and Fount of light,
> Dawn brightening the day....

Francis would have been familiar with sources such as these, which afforded him a Scriptural and liturgical background for describing Brother Sun as bearing the *significatione* of God.

Suggestions for Further Reading

Bodo, Murray, *Poetry as Prayer – St Francis of Assisi*, Phoenix Arizona, 2003; 2nd ed. 2015.

Brown, Raphael, *The Canticle of Brother Sun*, in Englebert, Omer, *St Francis of Assisi, a Biography*, transl. Cooper E.M., Chicago, 1966, Appendix VIII.

Delio, Ilia, *A Franciscan View of Creation*, New York, 2003.

Doyle, Eric, *St Francis and the Song of Brotherhood*, 1980; London, 1981.

Leclerc, Eloi, *The Canticle of Creatures, Symbols of Union*, transl. O'Connell M.J., Chicago, 1977.

OTHER PUBLISHED WORKS BY JOHN WATTS
ON FRANCISCAN SUBJECTS

A Canticle of Love – the Story of the Franciscan Sisters of the Immaculate Conception Edinburgh 2006;

A Tender Watering – Franciscans in Scotland from the Thirteenth to the Twenty-first Century Canterbury 2011;

A Beautiful Fragrance – the Story of Margaret Sinclair Edinburgh 2016;

The Story of Margaret Sinclair in Words and Pictures Edinburgh 2018.

OTHER WORKS ON FRANCISCAN SUBJECTS
PUBLISHED BY GRACEWING

Affair of the Heart – A Biblical and Franciscan Journey, Patricia Jordan FSM

Come Apart and Rest a While, Patricia Jordan FSM

Elizabeth Hayes – Pioneer Franciscan Journalist, Pauline Shaw MFIC

A Eucharistic Vision and the Spirituality of St Francis of Assisi, Mark of Whitstable OFM, Cap.

Francis and Thérèse – Great Little Saints, Patricia Jordan FSM

The Gift of St Francis, Jon Davis and Don McMonigle

Gospel Chivalry – Franciscan Romanticism, Mark of Whitstable OFM, Cap.

St Francis for Today, Edmund O'Gorman OFM, Conv.

Stabat Mater – The Mystery Hymn, Desmond Fisher